The Story of

Children in the
Second World War

Jane Shuter

 Raintree

www.raintreepublishers.co.uk
Visit our website to find out more information about **Raintree** books.

To order:
☎ Phone 44 (0) 1865 888112
🖹 Send a fax to 44 (0) 1865 314091
🖥 Visit the Raintree Bookshop at **www.raintreepublishers.co.uk** to browse our catalogue and order online.

First published in Great Britain by Raintree,
Halley Court, Jordan Hill, Oxford OX2 8EJ,
part of Pearson Education. Raintree is a registered
trademark of Pearson Education Ltd.

Editorial: Sian Smith
Design: Kimberley R. Miracle, Big Top and
 Joanna Hinton-Malivoire
Picture research: Ruth Blair
Production: Duncan Gilbert
Illustrated by Beehive illustration
Originated by Dot Gradations

Printed and bound in China by Leo Paper Group

ISBN 978 1 4062 1012 5 (hardback)
ISBN 978 1 4062 1022 4 (paperback)

12 11 10 09 08
10 9 8 7 6 5 4 3 2 1

British Library Cataloguing in Publication Data
Shuter, Jane
 The story of children in the Second World War
 1. World War, 1939-1945 - Children - Juvenile
literature
 I. Title

940.5'3161

Acknowledgments
The publishers would like to thank the following
for permission to reproduce photographs: ©Corbis
pp.6, 7, 13, 15, 16 (Bettmann) 10, 11, 12, 17
(Hulton-Deutsch Collection), 19 (Jerry Cooke);
©Getty Images pp. 8, 18 (Hulton Archive), 9
(Popperfoto); © TopFoto.co.uk p.14 (Public Record
Office, HIP)

Cover photograph of three young children during
evacuation reproduced with permission of ©Getty
Images (Hulton, Reg Speller)

Every effort has been made to contact copyright
holders of any material reproduced in this book.
Any omissions will be rectified in subsequent
printings if notice is given to the publisher.

Contents

Some words are printed in bold, **like this**. You can find out what they mean in the glossary.

The Second World War

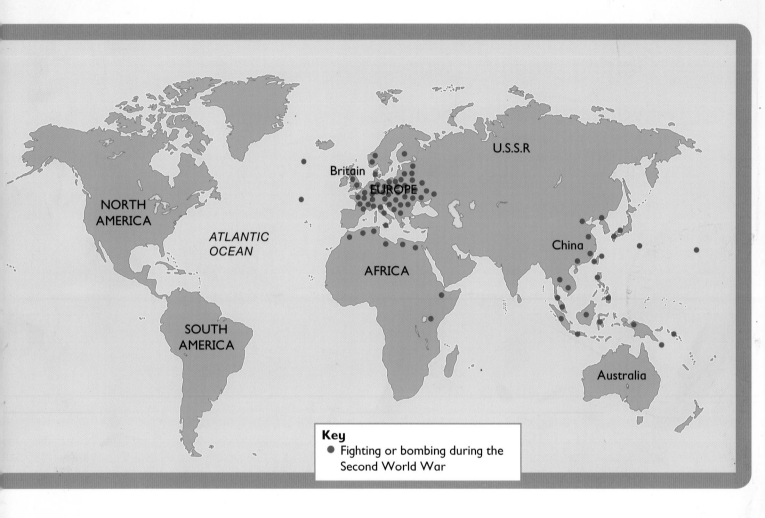

The Second World War began on 3 September 1939. Britain and France went to war to stop Germany **invading** other countries. As time passed, many different countries joined the war. So each side had **allies** who fought with them.

The Second World War in Europe went on until 7 May 1945. Britain and its allies won.

The Japanese, Germany's ally, carried on fighting. Finally, the Japanese gave in on 14 August 1945. The Second World War was over.

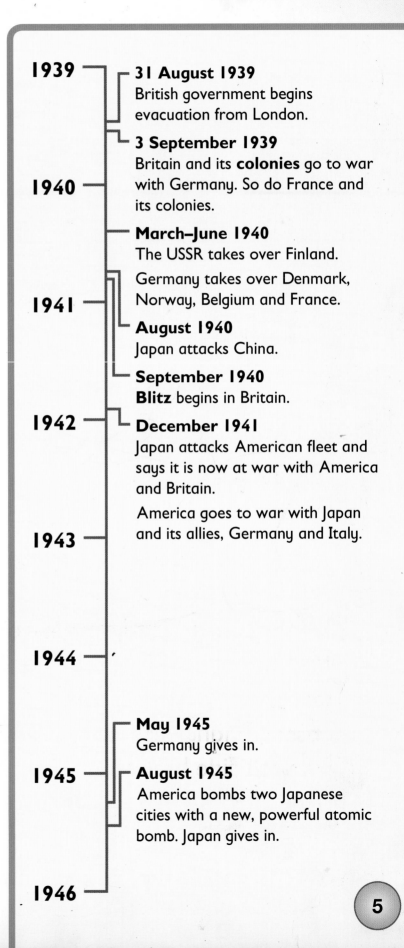

1939

31 August 1939
British government begins evacuation from London.

3 September 1939
Britain and its **colonies** go to war with Germany. So do France and its colonies.

1940

March–June 1940
The USSR takes over Finland.
Germany takes over Denmark, Norway, Belgium and France.

1941

August 1940
Japan attacks China.

September 1940
Blitz begins in Britain.

1942

December 1941
Japan attacks American fleet and says it is now at war with America and Britain.
America goes to war with Japan and its allies, Germany and Italy.

1943

1944

May 1945
Germany gives in.

1945

August 1945
America bombs two Japanese cities with a new, powerful atomic bomb. Japan gives in.

1946

Getting ready for war

Shelters were safe but scary places.

The British **government** thought the Germans would drop bombs on British cities as soon as the war started. They got ready for this before the war began. The government built big **air raid** shelters. People built shelters in their gardens, too.

People carried gas masks in a cardboard box.

The government told people to make **blackout** curtains for their homes. The curtains stopped any light from inside being seen outside. They turned off street lights at night. Everyone had to carry **gas masks**, too. This was in case the Germans dropped gas bombs.

Evacuate the children

Evacuees wore labels saying where they were going.

The **government** began to **evacuate** children even before the war began. They sent them from London to safer places, in the countryside.

Some **evacuees** went with their school. Others went by themselves.

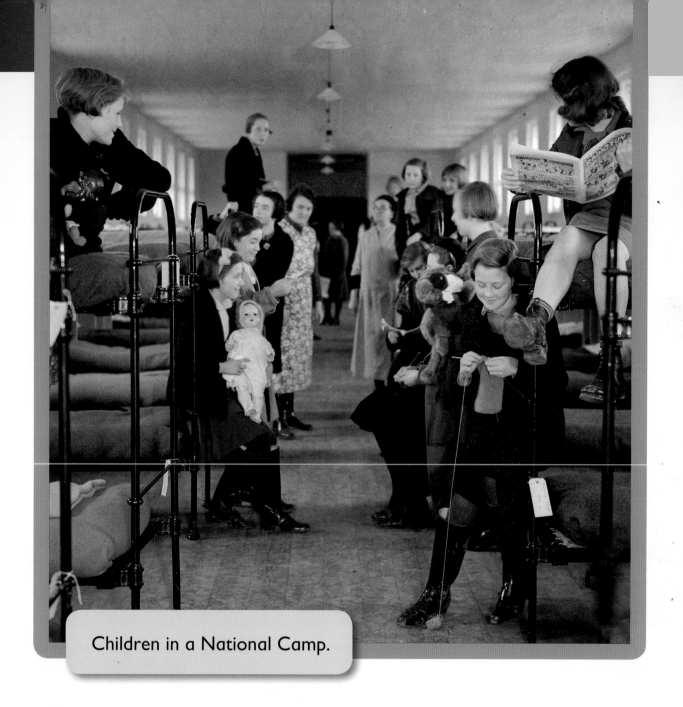

Children in a National Camp.

Some evacuees went to big National Camps run by the government. Others went to stay with **host families**. When evacuees arrived, a **billeting officer** took them to their host families.

Life as an evacuee

These boys have spent the day picking potatoes on a farm to help their host family.

Evacuees joined in life with their **host families**. Some evacuees stayed with one host family. Others lived with many different families. Not all families were kind to evacuees.

Evacuees who did not go home had Christmas parties together.

The Germans didn't bomb the cities at first. Many evacuees went home to their families for Christmas. Some did not return to their host families in the country. The **government** was not happy about this. They thought the Germans would bomb the cities soon.

The Blitz

Bombing in London.

The Germans began bombing Britain in July 1940. At first, they just bombed airfields, then railway lines and factories in cities.

In September 1940, they began to bomb cities heavily. This bombing was called the **Blitz**, from the German word *blitzkreig*, which means 'lightning war'.

Bombing in Berlin.

The Blitz bombing went on night after night. Many families who had not **evacuated** their children now sent them to safety. Children who stayed in the cities were in danger from the bombs. The British bombed German cities, so Germans evacuated their children too.

Rationing

A government poster from the war.

German **submarines** began to sink ships bringing food and weapons to Britain. The ships stopped coming. Many food supplies ran out. The British **government** told people to grow more vegetables and fruit. They even dug up parks to do this.

A woman swapping her ration coupons.

From January 1940, food and fuel were **rationed** in Britain. People could only buy a set amount of them. They were rationed in other countries fighting the war, too.

People had **ration books**. They swapped strips from the book for their rationed food and fuel.

Children in Europe

A Jewish family leave Memel, in Germany.

The **Nazi government** in Germany were cruel to many different groups of people. They hated Jewish people and passed laws against them. Many families wanted to send their children to safety. They sent them to live in another country as **refugees**.

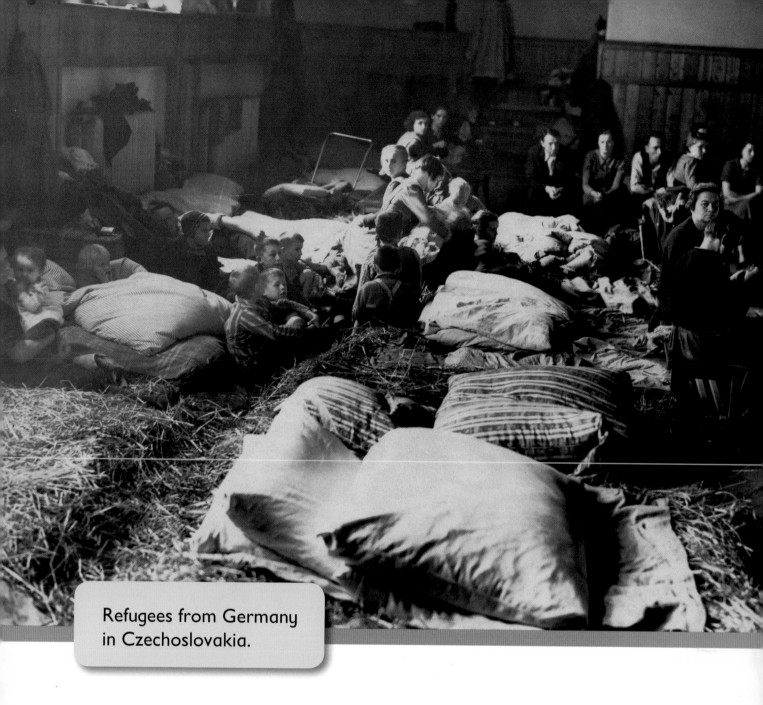

Refugees from Germany in Czechoslovakia.

Many families were not able to leave Europe as the German army took over more and more countries. Some of them became refugees without a safe place to stay. Many were caught and killed by the Nazis.

The war ends

Evacuees come home.

Fighting in Europe stopped in May 1945. Soldiers and **evacuees** started coming home.

Many homes had been bombed and people had nowhere to live. The **government** built lots of **prefabs**. These were **temporary** homes for people to live in until new homes could be built.

These children were still homeless in 1948.

Many thousands of people in Europe lost their homes or were separated from their families during the war. Some never found them again.

The war had caused a lot of damage and suffering. People wanted to make sure there was not another one.

Teachers' guide

These books have followed the QCA guidelines closely, but space has not allowed us to cover all the information and vocabulary the QCA suggest. Any suggested material not covered in the book is added to the discussion points below. The books can simply be read as information books, or they could be used as a focus for studying the unit. Below are discussion points grouped in pairs of pages, with suggested follow-up activities.

PAGES 4–5

Talk about:

- Stress government concerns about bombing and gas because these were used in the First World War and now planes could fly far enough for German planes carrying them to reach Britain.

- Explain the blackout, putting tape over windows to stop flying glass and the various kinds of shelters: big public ones, dug outs, Anderson shelters. Explain the home guard.

Possible activity:

- Use http://www.learningcurve.gov.uk/ homefront to see some of the preparations.

PAGES 8–9

Talk about:

- Explain that evacuation was never compulsory, but the government pressed people to send children away and to leave them there. Tell them that some children were "seavacuated" out of Britain, mostly to Canada. This stopped in 1941, after a German submarine sank a ship (only 13 of the 100 children on board survived).

Possible activity:

- Ask children to find out if any of their older relatives were evacuated and compile a survey. Design a poster to encourage parents to evacuate their children.

PAGES 10–11

Talk about:

- Stress that some evacuees had a great time, some had a terrible time; most had a reasonable time. It depended on the children, their host families and whether they went as a class with their teacher.

Possible activity:

- Hold an empathy brainstorm about being evacuated. Could discuss how they would feel generally or focus on just one small aspect. For example, they can take one small rucksack. What will they want to take (favourite toys, etc.)? What will their parents want them to take (warm clothes, etc.)?

PAGES 12–13

Talk about:

- Explain that the thing that made the Blitz different was that the bombing was heavy, it happened night after night and it targeted places where people lived and worked.

- Discuss the problems that heavy bombing like this created for people in European cities during (and after) the war.

Possible activity:

- Talk about the photos. One is Berlin, one is London. How do they know which is which?

PAGES 14–15

Talk about:

- Explain that what was rationed, and the size of the ration, varied. Essentials, such as food and fuel, were most tightly rationed. Germany had rationing too, and that varied as well. Tell them that rationing continued after the war. Bread was only rationed in Britain in 1946, after the war had ended.

Possible activity:

- http://allthatwomenwant.com/ wartimerecipes.htm has a recipe for carrot fudge that you could discuss or even make!

PAGES 16–17

Talk about:

- Stress that the war affected children in all the countries involved in the war – to varying extents. The Nazis persecuted groups other than Jewish people. They also shut German mentally and physically disabled people up in institutions where they were often used for experiments or left to die of neglect. Children in all these groups suffered.

Possible activity:

- Brainstorm the ways different countries might be affected (Britain had bombing, rationing, evacuation and so on. Australia had none of these, but sent people to fight and so children there would suffer from family members leaving and maybe being killed).

PAGES 18–19

Talk about:

- It is a QCA requirement that children should consider what has been done to try to stop another world war. At this age, it is only really possible to discuss the UN in a very general way. Since the guidelines were written, the wars in Iraq and Afghanistan have brought war closer to home, with many children having relatives affected in some way.

Possible activity:

- Debate possible ways to stop a future world war.

Local history work

You could do some work on how your area was affected by the war. Local libraries and museums will have resources to help. Some children should have relatives who were alive at the time, and so were involved in some way, who might be prepared to talk to the class.

Find out more

Books

Anne Frank, Harriet Castor and Helena Owen (Franklin Watts, 2001)

Children and the Blitz, Jane Shuter (Heinemann Library, 2004)

Home in the Blitz, Marilyn Tolhurst (A & C Black, 2000)

Websites

www.bbc.co.uk/history/ww2children/home.shtml
You can learn about war-time homes and rationing, look at posters, read letters written by soldiers and evacuees, and listen to radio clips and the sounds of war on this site.

http://www.iwm.org.uk/
Go to 'Learning resources' for information, games and activities to help you understand what life was like in World War II.

www.learningcurve.gov.uk/homefront
This website has videos and games that can help you to learn about evacuees, rationing and how people prepared for the war.

Glossary

air raid attack by many planes carrying bombs

allies people who are on the same side and agree to work together

billeting officer person who made sure that all the evacuees had a host family to go to

blackout making sure that no lights could been seen outside at night

Blitz short for *blitzkreig*, which means 'lightning war' in German. It was the nickname the British gave the German bombing of Britain and other cities in 1940–1941.

colonies parts of the world that a country controls

evacuate move people away from their home to somewhere safer

evacuee someone who is evacuated

gas mask mask worn over the head that makes poisonous air safe to breathe

government people who run a country

host family families who offered, or were made, to take evacuees into their homes

invade go into a country, with an army, to take it over

Nazi the Nazi Party ran Germany just before and during the Second World War

prefab short for 'prefabricated'. Prefab homes were homes that were made all the same size and shape in factories. They were quicker and cheaper to make than ordinary houses.

ration limit the amount of things that people can have

ration book book with pieces of paper to swap for things you can only have set amounts of

refugee person who has to leave the place they live, often quickly and taking very little, because it is no longer safe to live there

submarine machines that can move under the water. During the war they were used to fire underwater bombs at ships and other submarines.

temporary something that only lasts for a short time

Index